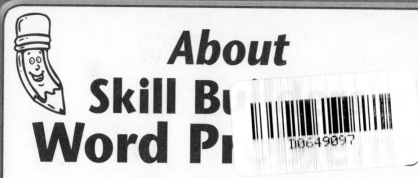

About
Skill Bu...
Word Pr...

by Carolyn Chapman

Welcome to RBP Books' Skill Builders series. Like our Summer Bridge Activities collection, the Skill Builders series is designed to make learning both fun and rewarding.

Students often ask their parents and teachers, "When am I ever going to use this?" Skill Builders Word Problems books have been developed to help students see the many uses of math in the world around them. The word problems in this book help students develop problem-solving skills in real-world situations while increasing confidence in their math skills.

Content for this book is based on current NCTM (National Council of Teachers of Mathematics) standards and supports what teachers are currently using in their classrooms. Word Problems can be used both at school and at home to engage students in problem solving.

The third-grade math skills used in this book include addition, sub-traction, multiplication, division, graphing, fractions, mea-surement, area and perimeter, time, and money values.

A critical thinking section includes exercises to help develop higher-order thinking skills.

Learning is more effective when approached with an element of fun and enthusiasm—just as most children approach life. That's why the Skill Builders combine entertaining and academically sound exercises with eye-catching graphics and fun themes—to make reviewing basic skills at school or home fun and effective, for both you and your budding scholars.

Table of Contents

Adding & Subtracting 2-Digit Numbers
Fishy Facts 3–4
Travel Time...............................5

Adding & Subtracting Whole Numbers
Movie Mania 6
Travel & Movie Review 7
Deli Delights.............................8
At the Zoo 9–10
Classroom Fun 11–12
Lunch Time!.......................13–14
Weather Highs & Lows 15

Adding & Subtracting 3- & 4-Digit Numbers
Geography Gems..............16–17
Time for Tunes.......................18

Adding & Subtracting Money
Gathering Groceries 19
Super Shoppers 20–21
What's for Dinner? 22
Earning and Spending 23

Multiplying 1-Digit Numbers
Safari Seekers...........................24
Lots of Cars 25
Safari & Cars Review................26

Multiplying 2-Digit Numbers
Pet Pals (no regrouping) 27
Growing & Mowing 28
Pet Pals & Growing Review 29
Painting Pals 30

Multiplying & Dividing
Bookworm Bonanza................31
Under the Sea....................32–33

Adding, Subtracting, & Multiplying Money
How Much Money? 34–35
Crazy Carnival....................36–37
Extra! Extra!............................38
Who Spends More? 39–40

Unit Conversions—Time
Are We There Yet? 41

Dividing by 1-Digit Numbers
Candy Store Sweets................42
Camping Out 43–44
Planting Perfect 45

Multiplication & Division Review
Party Planning 46–47

Drawing Pictures of Fractions
Picture Problems....................48

Adding & Subtracting Fractions
Pizza Party 49
At the Park 50
Pizza & Park Review................51
Painting Perfect 52
Cookie Cutters.......................53

Reading & Interpreting Tables & Graphs
Popsicles™ 54
Points Scored.........................55
Graph It!............................56–57
Up, Up, & Away 58–59
Through the Hoop 60

Finding Perimeter & Area
Measuring Up..........................61
Happy Helpers........................62

Practicing Mixed Skills
Fun at the Fair 63–64
Sports Store Sales 65–66
Sweet Treats 67

Critical Thinking Skills
Tiny-Tykes Toy Sales..........68–69
Class Pets.........................70–71
In the News! 72–73
At the Carnival 74

Answer Pages.......................75–80

Solve each problem.

Keshia has 37 goldfish in her aquarium. Mark has 19 in his aquarium. How many more goldfish does Keshia have than Mark?

```
  2 1
  3̶7
- 19
  18  goldfish
```

1. Jake has 58 guppies and 84 goldfish. How many fewer guppies than goldfish does Jake have?

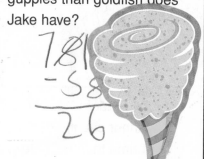

```
  7 8̶ 14̶
-   5 8
    2 6
```

2. Ben has 47 more goldfish than Leslie. Leslie has 73. How many goldfish does Ben have?

```
    1
   7 3
 + 4 7
 1 2 0
```

3. Isabel's aquarium has 43 plants. She took out 29 plants. How many plants does Isabel have left in her aquarium?

```
  3 4̶ 13̶
-   2 9
    1 4
```

4. Jamal's friend gave him 17 goldfish. He had 69 to start with. How many does he have now?

```
  8̶ 18̶
    7
  8 6
```

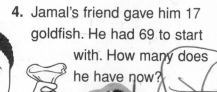

Fishy Facts

Solve each problem.

1. Denise has 93 comets in her aquarium. Jack has 35 comets in his aquarium. How many more comets does Denise have than Jack?

$$
\begin{array}{r}
8 \cancel{9}13 \\
-35 \\
\hline
58
\end{array}
$$

2. Marcus has guppies in his aquarium. Lucy has 17 more guppies than Marcus has. How many guppies does Lucy have?

$$
\begin{array}{r}
1 \\
25 \\
+17 \\
\hline
42
\end{array}
$$

3. Allie has 44 snails. Tanner has 11 more snails than Allie. How many snails do they have altogether?

$$
\begin{array}{r}
44 \\
+11 \\
\hline
55
\end{array}
$$

$$
\begin{array}{r}
44 \\
+55 \\
\hline
99
\end{array}
$$

4. Rob caught 73 shrimp. Tanner caught 25 fewer than Rob. How many did Tanner catch? How many shrimp did Rob and Tanner catch altogether?

$$
\begin{array}{r}
6 \\
7\cancel{1}3 \\
-25 \\
\hline
48
\end{array}
$$

$$
\begin{array}{r}
73 \\
+48 \\
\hline
121
\end{array}
$$

Did you know?

Fish have no eyelids. When you turn on the lights in a room, goldfish will swim for cover. They can't block out the light, so they will look for shelter among plants. Although goldfish can't close their eyes, they do sleep!

4

Travel Time

Choose numbers to fill in the blanks so that the answers are correct.

Paige sees <u>28</u> tourists with cameras and <u>29</u> tourists with binoculars. There are 57 tourists altogether.

$$\begin{array}{r} {}^{4}{}^{1}\\ \cancel{5}7 \\ -\ 28 \\ \hline 29 \end{array}$$

---

1. Ginger has ___ postcards. She mails ___ postcards. Now Ginger has 38 postcards left.

2. Mario drove ___ miles on Wednesday. On Thursday Jack drove ___ miles. Jack and Mario drove 97 miles altogether.

3. Jackson bought ___ souvenirs. His little sister broke ___ of the souvenirs. Jackson has 46 souvenirs left.

4. On Friday, Hector sells ___ maps to the movie stars' homes. On Saturday, Hector sells ___ maps. Hector sells 82 maps in all.

5

Movie Mania

Solve each problem.

Alexis sold 1,223 cups of Fizzy Cola. Sam sold 873 cups. How many cups of Fizzy Cola did Alexis and Sam sell altogether?

$$^1\!1,\!223$$
$$+\ 873$$
$$\overline{2,\!096}\ \textbf{cups}$$

1. In January, the theater sold 5,685 movie tickets. The theater sold 183 more movie tickets in March than in January. How many tickets were sold in March?

2. Bill sold 127 boxes of Starblast candy and 839 packages of licorice. How many more packages of licorice than Starblast candy did Bill sell?

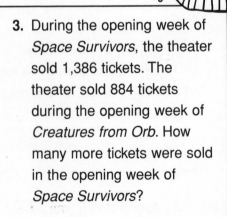

3. During the opening week of *Space Survivors*, the theater sold 1,386 tickets. The theater sold 884 tickets during the opening week of *Creatures from Orb*. How many more tickets were sold in the opening week of *Space Survivors*?

4. The ShowTime Theater has 1,253 seats. The Cinemania Theater has 784 seats. How many more seats does the ShowTime Theater have than the Cinemania Theater?

Solve each problem.

1. Caroline buys a poster from every city she visits. On her first trip she buys ___ posters. On her second trip she buys ___ posters. She now has 57 posters.

2. Emily drives a tour bus. She drives ___ tourists to the beach and ___ tourists to the canyon. In all, Emily drives 74 tourists to the beach or the canyon.

3. Lizzy sold 468 small buckets of popcorn, and Ted sold 245 large buckets of popcorn. How many buckets were sold altogether?

4. The ShowTime Theater has 962 tickets available for Monday night. They sell 543 tickets. How many tickets do they have left?

Did you know?

The hottest temperature recorded in the U.S. was 134° F. It was recorded in Death Valley, CA, on July 10, 1913. The coldest temperature recorded in the U.S. was ⁻80° F. It was recorded at Prospect Creek, AK, on January 23, 1971.

Deli Delights

Solve each problem.

Tami ordered 49 sandwiches from the deli. She ordered 12 cheese sandwiches and 22 meatball sandwiches. The rest were turkey. How many turkey sandwiches did she order?

$$\begin{array}{r} 12 \\ + 22 \\ \hline 34 \end{array} \qquad \begin{array}{r} 49 \\ - 34 \\ \hline 15 \end{array} \text{ turkey sandwiches}$$

1. Mark made 58 sandwiches at the deli during lunchtime. He made 16 peanut butter sandwiches, 14 tuna sandwiches, and 12 egg salad sandwiches. The rest were ham. How many ham sandwiches did Mark make?

2. Jose bought 19 sandwiches, 24 sodas, and 18 bags of chips. How many items did he buy in all? If everyone who got a soda wanted chips, how many more bags of chips would Jose need?

3. Max used 85 loaves of bread in one week. He used 25 loaves on Monday, 17 on Tuesday, and 21 on Wednesday. How many loaves did he use the rest of the week?

4. Susan should have had 134 items. She has 36 sandwiches, 33 bags of chips, and 48 sodas. How many items did Susan forget?

8

Solve each problem.

Anita saw 12 parakeets, 4 parrots, 2 cocka-
toos, and some sparrows. If she
saw 19 birds altogether, how
many sparrows did she see?

$$
\begin{array}{r}
12 \\
4 \\
+\ 2 \\
\hline
18
\end{array}
\qquad
\begin{array}{r}
19 \\
-\ 18 \\
\hline
1\ \textbf{sparrow}
\end{array}
$$

---

1. Jack cleaned 25 animal
cages in one week. He
cleaned 4 cages on Monday,
6 cages on Tuesday, and 11
cages on Wednesday.
How many cages did
he clean the rest of
the week?

2. Ryan likes the reptile house.
He saw 10 reptiles
altogether. If he saw
2 chameleons and 4 lizards,
how many snakes did
he see?

---

3. The lions and tigers ate 24
pounds of meat in 3 months.
If they ate 9 pounds the first
month and 8 pounds the
second month, how many
pounds of meat did they eat
the third month?

4. Sixty-three people visited
the monkey house during
the week. There were 7
visitors on Friday and 11 on
Saturday. How many people
visited during the rest of the
week?

9

At the Zoo

Solve each problem.

1. Lucy added 6 gallons of water to the penguin pond on Monday. On both Tuesday and Wednesday she added another 12 gallons. The pond now has 49 gallons of water. How much water did it have to start with?

2. Marcy counted 28 snakes during her visits to the zoo. On her first trip, she counted 9 snakes. On her second trip, she counted 6. How many snakes did she count on her third trip?

3. Tim fed the elephants 7 pounds of food on Tuesday, 8 pounds on Wednesday, and 4 pounds on Thursday. If Tim had 49 pounds of food to start with, how much food does he have left?

4. Jan took pictures of 37 mammals at the zoo. She took 7 pictures of bears, 5 pictures of lions, and 2 pictures of zebras. How many pictures of other mammals did Jan take?

Did you know?

The prefix *centi-* means 100. So a centimeter is one 100th of a meter. However, *centipedes* don't always have 100 legs. Some centipedes can be a foot long and have more than 300 legs. Others are only about an inch long with 70 legs.

Classroom Fun

Solve each problem.

There are 540 students in Julie's class. 239 students have blue
notebooks, 94 have purple notebooks,
and 118 have green notebooks. The rest
have red notebooks. How many students
have red notebooks?

$$\begin{array}{r} {}^{1\,2}\\ 239\\ 94\\ +118\\ \hline 451 \end{array} \qquad \begin{array}{r} {}^{4\,13\,1}\\ 540\\ -451\\ \hline 89 \end{array} \text{ red}$$

notebooks

1. Mr. Peterson graded 244
   papers in 4 months. He
   graded 46 papers during the
   first month, 73 during the
   second month, and 64
   during the third month. How
   many papers did he grade
   during the fourth month?

2. Amy's class used 23 pencils
   in March, 43 pencils in April,
   and 39 pencils in May. If
   there were 950 pencils to
   start with, how many pencils
   are left?

3. Oakwood Elementary has
   543 students. There are 43
   students in the third grade
   and 54 students in the fourth
   grade. How many
   students are in the
   other grades?

4. In Jenny's class, 13 students
   have green eyes. Twelve
   students have blue eyes.
   The rest have brown eyes.
   If there are 48 students in
   Jenny's class, how many
   have brown eyes?

11

Classroom Fun

Solve each problem.

1. Students in Eric's class voted on their favorite cookie: chocolate chip, raisin, or peanut butter. If 113 people voted for chocolate chip and 32 voted for raisin, how many voted for peanut butter if 263 people voted in all?

2. Susan counted 875 backpacks in her school. If she counted 533 blue backpacks, 139 red backpacks, and the rest were orange, how many orange backpacks did she count?

3. At Smithfield School, 109 students play on teams. Eighteen students play basketball, 22 students play volleyball, and 54 play softball. The rest play soccer. How many students play soccer?

4. There are 321 math books and 1,684 reading books in the school. The rest of the books are science books. If there are 3,514 books altogether, how many are science books?

Did you know?

The first known printed book came from China. It was made with wooden blocks dipped in ink in about A.D. 868. Printing was slow and impractical until Johannes Gutenberg invented a way to print books with moveable metal blocks almost 600 years ago.

Solve the problems using the information in the table.

How many more calories does a hamburger and French fries have than one slice of pizza?

FOOD ITEMS	CALORIES
applesauce	104
chicken noodle soup	145
chocolate chip cookie	126
hamburger	369
French fries	237
milk	95
banana	75
pizza (1 slice)	378

hamburger   369
French fries + 237
         = 606 calories
pizza − 378
         = 228 calories

1. James eats a banana and a glass of milk. Katie eats chicken noodle soup and milk. How many more calories did Katie have than James?

2. Kyle eats a hamburger, a glass of milk, and a chocolate chip cookie. How many calories does Kyle eat altogether?

Tuna on rye—my favorite!

13

Lunch Time!

Solve each problem using the table on page 13.

1. Oscar eats 2 bowls of chicken noodle soup. Caroline eats applesauce and 2 chocolate chip cookies. How many more calories does Caroline eat than Oscar?

2. If Jeff eats 2 slices of pizza, and Kim eats 1 chocolate chip cookie and a hamburger, how many more calories does Jeff eat?

3. For breakfast, Amber has a banana and 2 glasses of milk. For lunch, she eats a slice of pizza. How many more calories does Amber eat for lunch than for breakfast?

4. Rex ate 599 calories. If he had applesauce and a chocolate chip cookie, what was the last thing he ate?

Did you know?

It takes about a whole day for your body to digest the food you eat. Digestion starts in the mouth with chewing and saliva, and it ends in the intestines. If you uncoiled your intestines, they could be up to 30 feet long!

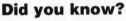

14

Solve each problem.

> The highest temperature in Duluth, Minnesota, was 97° F. The highest temperature in Barrow, Alaska, was 79° F. How much warmer was Duluth than Barrow?
>
>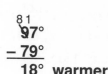
>
> 8 1
> **97°**
> **− 79°**
> **18° warmer**
>
>

1. Seattle, Washington, received 37 inches of rain in a year. Jackson, Mississippi, had 55 inches of rain. How much more rain did Jackson get than Seattle?

2. The maximum normal temperature in January for Houston, Texas, is 61° F. Rapid City, South Dakota, has a maximum normal temperature of 34° F in January. How much colder is Rapid City than Houston?

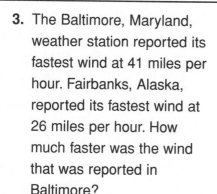

3. The Baltimore, Maryland, weather station reported its fastest wind at 41 miles per hour. Fairbanks, Alaska, reported its fastest wind at 26 miles per hour. How much faster was the wind that was reported in Baltimore?

4. In July, Los Angeles, California's, highest temperature was 84° F. Its lowest temperature during the same month was 65° F. What was the difference between its highest and lowest temperature?

Word Problems Grade 3—RBP0709

Geography Gems

Solve each problem.

In Hawaii, the Kilauea volcano is 4,190 feet high. The Mount St. Helens volcano, located in Washington, is 8,364 feet high. How much higher is Mount St. Helens than Kilauea?

$$\begin{array}{r} 8,\overset{2\,1}{3}64 \\ -\ 4,190 \\ \hline 4,174 \text{ feet} \end{array}$$

1. In the Caribbean Sea, the island of Barbados covers 166 square miles. The island of Jamaica measures 4,244 square miles. How many total square miles make up Barbados and Jamaica together?

2. The average depth of the Red Sea is 1,764 feet. The average depth of the Black Sea is 3,906 feet. How much deeper is the Black Sea than the Red Sea on average?

3. Castle Peak and Pikes Peak are both located in Colorado. Castle Peak is 14,265 feet high. Pikes Peak is 14,110. How much taller is Castle Peak?

4. The island of Hawaii measures 4,028 square miles. The island of Oahu is 600 square miles. How much larger is the island of Hawaii than Oahu?

Geography Gems

Solve each problem.

1. Salt Lake City, Utah, has an altitude of 4,266 feet. Tulsa, Oklahoma, has an altitude of 804 feet. How much higher is Salt Lake City than Tulsa?

2. Lake Erie is 241 miles long. Lake Ontario is 193 miles long. How long are Lake Erie and Lake Ontario altogether?

3. Brazil has 338 endangered plants. Peru has 269 endangered plants, and Jamaica has 206. How many more endangered plants do Jamaica and Peru have altogether than Brazil?

4. Samoa has an area of 2,934 square kilometers. Tonga has an area of 750 square kilometers. How much larger is Samoa than Tonga?

Did you know?

One of the world's most active volcanoes is located in Hawaii. Since January 3, 1983, Kilauea has been erupting continuously. It has destroyed over 180 homes.

17

Time for Tunes

Lisa's class took a poll at their school. They asked students what type of music they liked best. Use the results below to answer the questions that follow.

| How many total students like pop music or country music?

$\overset{1\ 11}{3,493}$
$\underline{+\ 1,998}$
5,491 students | **Rosewood School's**
Favorite Music Poll

Rock   4,755 students
Pop   3,493 students
Country 1,998 students
Rap   1,043 students
Jazz   845 students
Oldies   391 students
Classical 173 students |

1. How many more students like rap music than jazz music?

2. How many total students like oldies music or classical music?

3. More students like rock music than pop music. How many more students like rock music?

4. How many students like jazz music or oldies music altogether?

Gathering Groceries

Use the price list below to answer each question.

Eric's mom wants him to buy 1 gallon of milk and 3 boxes of cereal. How much money does he need?

$$\begin{array}{r} \overset{1\ 1}{\$2.89} \\ +\ \$10.79 \\ \hline \$13.68 \end{array}$$

Grocery List

1 bag of carrots	$1.79
1 package of grapes	$2.47
2 pounds of chicken	$6.62
1 gallon of milk	$2.89
3 loaves of bread	$3.58
8 cups of yogurt	$4.27
1 package of cheese	$5.59
3 boxes of cereal	$10.79
1 package of gum	$.76

1. Kendra buys 1 package of cheese. She pays for the cheese with a ten-dollar bill. How much change will Kendra get back?

Cheese 1

2. Daniel buys 8 cups of yogurt and 3 loaves of bread. How much does Daniel spend altogether?

3. Kim has $15.25. She buys 2 pounds of chicken. How much does she have left?

4. Marc buys 1 package of grapes and 3 loaves of bread. His little sister wants a package of gum. Marc only has $7.00 in his wallet. Does he have enough money to buy the gum?

19

Super Shoppers

Solve each problem using the prices below for each item.

Remember to put the "$" sign in your answer.

Lisa buys a soda and the markers. How much does she spend?

$$\begin{array}{r} \overset{1}{\$1.25} \\ + \ \$6.45 \\ \hline \$7.70 \end{array}$$

soda	$1.25
comic book	$3.75
pretzel	$2.36
T-shirt	$5.27
candy	$2.65
markers	$6.45
socks	$7.50
CD	$14.87

1. How much more does the comic book cost than the candy?

2. Jason has $10.00. If he buys a T-shirt, how much money will he have left?

3. How much will Emily spend if she buys socks and a pretzel?

4. Henry wants a new comic book, but he only has $1.63. How much more money does Henry need to buy the comic book?

20

Solve each problem.

Mike has $20.53 in his wallet. He spent $5.88 on baseball cards and $11.47 on a CD. How much did he have to start with?

$$\begin{array}{r} {}^{1\ 1}\ \\ \$20.53 \\ 5.88 \\ + 11.47 \\ \hline \$37.88 \end{array}$$ **to start with**

1. Alex spends $13.95 for a CD. Then he spends $5.39 for lunch. On his way out of the mall, he spends $7.45 at the arcade. If Alex started with $30.00 in his wallet, how much does he have left?

2. Gary has $7.35 left in his wallet. He spent $38.43 at the grocery store, $20.05 for gas, and $65.97 for car repairs. How much did Gary start with?

3. Jean has $60.00. She buys a book for $22.43 and a pair of shoes for $34.88. How much money does she have left?

4. Sarah has $1.24 in her pocket. She spent $7.93 at the video store, $5.48 on stickers, and $8.83 on candy. How much did she start with?

21

What's for Dinner?

Solve each problem using the prices below..

Leslie buys a soda and a hurricane hot dog. How much does she spend? Leslie pays for her dinner with a ten-dollar bill. How much change will she get back?

HARRY'S Hamburger Hut

Home of the Jungle Burger!

soda	$1.49
native nachos	$4.75
jungle burger	$3.49
fries	$2.39

hurricane hot dog	$3.55
tropical twist shake	$3.75
crunch 'n munch meal	$28.55

TRY IT!

Crunch 'N Munch Meal

$$\begin{array}{r} {\scriptstyle 1\ 1} \\ \$1.49 \\ +\ \$3.55 \\ \hline \$5.04 \end{array}$$

$$\begin{array}{r} {\scriptstyle 9\ 9\ 1} \\ \$\cancel{10.00} \\ -\ \$5.04 \\ \hline \$4.96 \end{array}$$

1. Eric has $15.00. If he buys the native nachos and a tropical twist shake, how much money will he have left?

2. How much will Ashley spend if she buys a jungle burger and a soda?

3. Sam's family orders a crunch 'n munch meal. Sam orders a tropical twist shake. Sam's mom has only $30.00. How much more money does she need?

4. How much more does the hurricane hot dog cost than the jungle burger?

Earning and Spending

Solve each problem.

1. Jamal earns $15.00 raking lawns. Then he buys a toy car for $4.69 and a candy bar for $1.79. How much does he have left?

2. Ramona earns $22.97 babysitting. She spends $3.94 for stickers, $1.98 for candy, and $5.83 for socks. How much does she have left?

3. Doug earns $5.00 for each lawn he mows. He mows 3 lawns and then buys a birthday present for his sister that costs $6.43. How much does he have left?

4. Amanda is saving her money for a scooter that costs $30.00. She earned $8.95 for babysitting, $12.00 for cleaning the garage, and $5.50 for taking care of the neighbor's cat. How much more does she need to buy the scooter?

Did you know?

The first metal coin may have come from Turkey about 670 B.C. In 1950, the Diners' Club introduced the first credit card.

Safari Seekers

Lori is on a safari to observe animals. She's keeping a diary of the things she sees. Help her finish writing about what she has seen.

Lori sees 3 times as many giraffes as elephants. Lori sees 6 elephants. How many giraffes does Lori see?

3
x 6
18 giraffes

1. Lori and her group travel in jeeps while looking at the animals. Each jeep has 4 seats. There are 7 jeeps in the group. How many people are in Lori's group if all of the seats are filled?

2. Lori is watching 2 spiders crawling in the dirt. The brown spider crawls twice as far as the black spider. The black spider crawls 3 feet. How far does the brown spider crawl?

There's a lot of math on a safari!

3. Each day, Lori drinks 3 bottles of water. How many bottles of water will Lori drink in a week?

4. Lori sees 4 herds of wildebeest. Each herd has 9 wildebeest. How many wildebeest does Lori see?

Lots of Cars

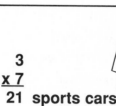

Solve each problem.

Jasmine is buying a sports car.
There are 3 rows of sports
cars with 7 cars in each row.
How many sports cars are
there in all?

$$\begin{array}{r} 3 \\ \times\,7 \\ \hline 21 \end{array}$$ **sports cars**

1. Each car has 4 tires. There are 9 cars. How many tires are there altogether?

2. Morgan wants to test drive a car and needs the key. Each key ring has 6 keys. If there are 9 key rings, how many keys are there total?

3. Chloe wants a new truck. The car dealer has 7 times as many trucks as cars. The car dealer has 8 cars. How many trucks does the car dealer have?

4. Sara likes red cars. The Motor Madness car lot has 5 times as many red cars as the Speeds-a-Lot car lot. The Speeds-a-Lot car lot has 8 red cars. How many red cars are on the Motor Madness car lot?

Word Problems Grade 3—RBP0709

Solve each problem.

1. In the evening, Lori helps set up camp. There are 3 rows with 8 tents in each row. How many tents are there?

2. Jason sees 4 times as many sport utility vehicles as sports cars. Jason sees 3 sports cars. How many sport utility vehicles does Jason see?

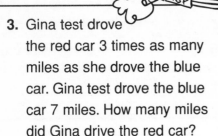

3. Gina test drove the red car 3 times as many miles as she drove the blue car. Gina test drove the blue car 7 miles. How many miles did Gina drive the red car?

4. Stan uses 2 bottles of car polish on his car every month. How many bottles of car polish will Stan use in 9 months?

Did you know?
A cheetah can run twice as fast as a giraffe. The cheetah can run up to 70 miles per hour.

Pet Pals

Emmett is helping his brother in the pet store after school. Help him find the answer to each problem.

Emmett is going to feed the rabbits. There are 11 cages with 4 rabbits in each cage. How many rabbits will Emmett need to feed?

11
x 4
44 rabbits

1. The pet store sells 2 times as many red pet collars as blue pet collars. Emmett sells 42 blue pet collars. How many red pet collars does Emmett sell?

2. The pet store has 21 turtles. Emmett feeds 2 lettuce leaves to each turtle. How many lettuce leaves does Emmett feed the turtles?

3. Emmett helps take the dogs for a walk. The pet store has 3 times as many poodles as cocker spaniels. It has 13 cocker spaniels. How many poodles does the pet store have?

4. Emmett is ordering more canary seed for the pet store. If the canaries eat 4 bags of seed in a month, how many bags will Emmett need to order for the next 12 months?

Word Problems Grade 3—RBP0709

Growing and Mowing

Solve each problem.

Max needs 48 pounds of grass seed for each lawn he plants. If Max plants 3 lawns, how many pounds of grass seed will he need?

$$\begin{array}{r} {\scriptstyle 2} \\ 48 \\ \times\ 3 \\ \hline 144 \end{array}$$ **pounds of seed**

1. Spencer is planting tomato plants. He plants 5 rows of 47 tomato plants. How many tomato plants does Spencer plant altogether?

2. Lizzie has 17 watering cans. Each watering can holds 6 gallons of water. How many gallons of water will Lizzie need to fill all 17 watering cans?

3. Jess is putting fertilizer on 23 lawns. He needs 4 bags of fertilizer for each lawn. How many bags of fertilizer will Jess need to buy?

4. Sara is mowing lawns for the summer. She mows 5 lawns each week. If Sara mows lawns for 23 weeks, how many lawns will she mow altogether?

Solve each problem.

1. The iguanas eat 3 times per week. How many times will Emmett need to feed the iguanas in the next 32 weeks?

2. Emmett sells 3 times as many dog toys as cat toys. Emmett sells 23 cat toys. How many dog toys does Emmett sell?

3. Kyle has 3 times as many garden tools as Anne. Anne has 37 garden tools. How many garden tools does Kyle have?

4. Josh plants 59 squash plants. Each plant has 6 squashes growing on the vine. How many squashes does Josh have?

Did you know?

While a cat is sleeping, its body temperature drops slightly. This explains why some cats like to sleep next to their owner or in the sunlight where it is warmer.

Iguanas have a third eye located on the top of their head. The third eye is called a parietal eye. It can detect light and darkness, but not colors.

Painting Pals

Solve each problem.

Tyler has 34 tubes of white paint. He has 7 times as many tubes of yellow paint. How many tubes of paint does Tyler have altogether?	34 x 7 238 tubes of yellow paint + 34 tubes of white paint 272 **tubes of paint**

1. Linus has 62 gallons of red paint. He has 9 times as many gallons of green paint. How many gallons of paint does Linus have altogether?

2. Henry painted 34 feet of fence on Tuesday. On Wednesday, he painted 5 times as many feet as on Tuesday. If Henry has 400 feet to paint, how many feet of fence does he have left to paint?

3. Dora ordered 188 small paintbrushes. She ordered 7 times as many large brushes as small brushes. How many paintbrushes did Dora order altogether?

4. Gina is using leftover paint to paint her wall. She has 15 liters of yellow paint. She has 6 times as many liters of white paint. If she needs 110 liters of paint, will she have enough?

Bookworm Bonanza

Solve each problem.

> Hilary reads 842 pages a week. How many pages will Hilary read in 9 weeks?
>
> $$\begin{array}{r} {\scriptstyle 3\ 1} \\ \mathbf{842} \\ \underline{\times\ \ 9} \\ \mathbf{7,578} \ \textbf{pages} \end{array}$$

1. Each day, 328 people come to the library. How many people will come to the library in a week?

2. Each magazine box holds 9 magazines. The library has 528 full magazine boxes. How many magazines does the library have?

Wait 'til the critics see these!

3. Gary checked out 467 books in a year. Kristen checked out 3 times as many books as Gary. How many books did Kristen check out?

4. The Southtown Library has 8 times as many books as the Littleton Library. The Littleton Library has 356 books. How many books does the Southtown Library have?

Under the Sea

Solve each problem.

Madison saw 14 yellow fish. She saw 8 times as many blue fish as yellow fish. How many fish did she see altogether?	**14** **x 8** **112** **+ 14** **126 fish altogether**

1. Amanda collected 19 pink seashells and 16 white seashells. If she has 5 boxes and puts the same number in each box, how many are in each box?

2. Divers saw 49 tropical fish on their first dive. They saw 6 times more tropical fish on their second dive. How many fish did they see altogether?

3. Rhonda collected 31 seashells. Gary collected 5 times as many seashells as Rhonda. How many seashells did Rhonda and Gary collect altogether?

4. A blue whale traveled 36 feet the first time it was sighted. The second time it was sighted, the blue whale had traveled 4 times as far as the first time. How far did the blue whale travel altogether?

Under the Sea

Solve each problem.

1. Max saw 87 fish while diving. Rita saw 6 times as many fish as Max. How many more fish did Rita see than Max?

2. The dolphin swims 42 feet. The shark swims 5 times as far as the dolphin. How many more feet does the shark swim than the dolphin?

3. Tim saw 13 octopi and 19 sea urchins. If he saw 6 times as many tropical fish as sea urchins, how many underwater creatures did Tim see altogether?

4. Gabrielle studied 38 fish in March. In April, she studied 8 times as many as in March. How many more fish did Gabrielle study in April than in March?

Did you know?

Some scientists estimate that if you took all the salt from the ocean, it would make a layer 500 feet thick over the whole earth.

How Much Money?

Solve each problem.

Max has $8.32 in his pocket. What coins
and bills could Max have?

**1 five-dollar bill, 3 one-dollar bills,
1 quarter, 1 nickel, and 2 pennies**

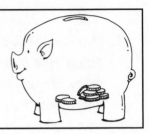

1. Tia has 3 one-dollar bills, 2
quarters, and 1 dime in her
piggy bank. How much
money does Tia have?

2. Mr. Cardoza is buying
doughnuts for his class. The
doughnuts cost $13.49. He
has 1 ten-dollar bill, 3 one-
dollar bills, and 2 quarters in
his wallet. Does he have
enough money to pay for the
doughnuts?

3. Tanner has 2 five-dollar bills,
4 dimes, and 2 nickels in his
wallet. How much money
does Tanner have in all?

4. Sheena has $11.76 in her
bank. What coins and bills
could Sheena have?

Solve each problem.

1. Peg has 3 ten-dollar bills, 3 quarters, and 5 nickels. How much money does she have?

2. Jackson has 2 one-dollar bills, 8 dimes, and 3 pennies in his pocket. How much money does Jackson have in all?

3. Annie needs $8.75 to buy her school supplies. She has 1 five-dollar bill, 3 one-dollar bills, 2 quarters and a dime in her purse. Does she have enough money to buy her school supplies?

4. Denise has $17.43 in her bank. What coins and bills could Denise have?

I'm saving my money for summer vacation!

Did you know?

In the year 2000, a total of 23.3 million Harry Potter books were sold in the United States.

Solve each problem.

Isabella buys 7 balloons for
35¢ each. How much does
she spend in all?

```
  3
.35
x 7
$2.45
```

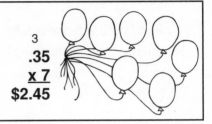

1. Tyler, Ann, and Jason want
to get their faces painted.
Face painting costs 69¢.
How much money will the 3
of them need to have their
faces painted?

2. Carl buys 256 tickets for 3¢
each. How much does he
spend on tickets?

3. Charlotte rides the Spin-a-
Whirl 19 times. If 1 ride
costs 5¢, how much does
Charlotte spend on Spin-a-
Whirl rides altogether?

4. Jess buys 146 pieces of
candy for 6¢ each. How
much does he spend in all?

36

Crazy Carnival

Solve each problem.

1. T-shirts cost $18 each.
   Amy buys 7 T-shirts.
   How much does Amy spend
   on T-shirts?

2. Nick buys 5 slices of pizza.
   Each slice of pizza costs
   89¢. How much does Nick
   spend on pizza?

3. At the Toss-a-Ring
   game, each ring costs
   3¢. Erin buys 76 rings.
   How much does she
   spend?

4. Erica has 9 friends. She
   buys each friend a
   soda for 79¢ each.
   How much does she
   spend on sodas?

Did you know?

October is National Pizza Month. Americans eat almost 100 acres
of pizza a day!

Extra! Extra!

Solve each problem.

Jonathan delivers 9 newspapers. He gets paid $1.14 for each newspaper he delivers. How much money does Jonathan earn?

```
  1 3
$1.14
x   9
$10.26
```

1. Annie places an ad in the newspaper. The newspaper charges 5¢ a word. Annie's ad has 694 words. How much does the ad cost?

2. Denise spends $34.56 at the newsstand. Meg spends $58.31 at the newsstand. How much more money does Meg spend than Denise?

3. The *Daily Times* sells 3,491 newspapers for 4¢ each. How much money does the *Daily Times* make?

4. Tara buys 2 newspapers that cost $3.95 each. She gives the clerk $10.00. How much change does Tara get back?

38

Who Spends More?

Solve each problem using the price tags.

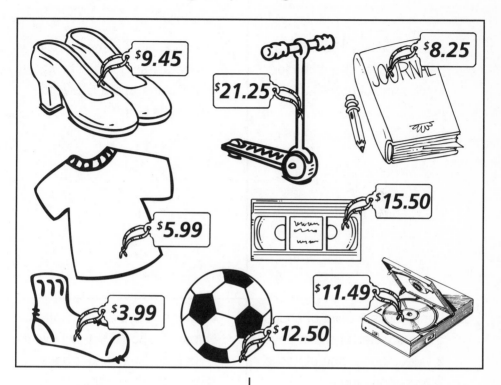

1. Erica buys a pair of shoes and a CD. Alex buys 2 videos. Who spends more?

2. Sam buys 3 T-shirts, a pair of shoes, and 1 pair of socks. Liz buys a scooter. Who spends more?

Who Spends More?

Solve each problem using the price tags on page 39.

1. Jessica buys a book and a pair of socks. She stops for lunch and spends $4.39. Isaac buys a CD and 2 books. Who spends more?

2. Lance buys a soccer ball and a T-shirt. Mitch buys 2 T-shirts and a CD. Who spends more?

3. Penny buys 2 pairs of shoes and a scooter. Jackson buys 3 videos and a pair of socks. Who spends more?

4. Megan buys 2 books and a pair of shoes. Marcy buys a pair of shoes and 2 pairs of socks. Who spends more?

Did you know?
A dime has 118 ridges along its edge. A quarter has 119. A nickel has none.

Are We There Yet?

Chloe and her family are taking a vacation. Help her solve the following problems.

Chloe's family waits for her brother to get home. It's 6:00, and they wait for 30 minutes. What time is it now?

6:00 + :30 = 6:30

1. Chloe's family leaves at 7:15. They drive for 30 minutes and then stop for dinner. What time is it when they stop for dinner?

2. At 8:45, Chloe asks how much longer it will take to get to their hotel. Her mom says it will take 1 hour and 30 minutes more. What time will they reach their hotel?

3. At 9:00, Chloe's little brother needs to stop for a break. The family stops for 15 minutes. What time do they get back on the road again?

4. Chloe sets her alarm clock for 7:15 in the morning. She oversleeps 30 minutes. What time does Chloe get up?

Candy Store Sweets

Solve each problem.

Henry, Misha, and Ann buy a package of licorice. There are 12 pieces of licorice in the package. How many pieces will each person get?

4 pieces of licorice

3) 12

1. The jar of jawbreakers has 20 pieces. Four customers buy equal numbers of jaw-breakers until the jar is empty. How many pieces did each customer buy?

2. A case of candy bars con-tains 72 bars. There are 9 boxes in a case. How many candy bars are in each box?

3. Dotty, Jackson, and Susan share a package of gum-drops equally. If the package contains 18 gumdrops, how many will each person get?

4. Mason gives 42 packages of Tart-n-Tangies to 7 friends to share equally. How many packages of Tart-n-Tangies does each of his friends get?

Candy, candy!

42

Solve each problem.

Camp Oakwood has 120 campers. If there are 5 campers in each tent, how many tents are there?

```
      24 tents
  5 ) 120
     -10
      20
     -20
       0
```

1. Megan has a package of 376 marshmallows. If each camper roasts 8 marshmallows, how many campers can roast marshmallows?

2. Dave has a case of 228 flashlights. There are 3 boxes in a case. How many flashlights are in each box?

3. Tim made 588 sandwiches for the campers in 1 week. How many sandwiches did Tim make each day?

4. Denise has 365 packages of trail mix. She puts 5 packages in each backpack. How many backpacks does she fill?

I love camping!

Solve each problem.

1. Kendra has 276 inches of string. She cuts the string into 6-inch pieces for making bracelets. How many 6-inch pieces of string can she cut?

2. Shannon has 585 gallons of punch. If the campers use 9 gallons of punch per day, how many days will the punch last?

3. Camp Hillcrest has 189 campers. If 7 sleeping bags fit in 1 tent, how many tents will Camp Hillcrest need?

4. Rob cooked 108 strips of bacon. Each camper ate 3 strips of bacon. How many campers ate bacon?

Did you know?
One of the largest balls of string is in Darwin, Minnesota. It weighs 17,400 pounds, is 12 feet in diameter, and was rolled up by one man.

Planting Perfect

Solve each problem.

> Katie has 11 daisies and 7 roses. If she
> puts 3 flowers in each vase, how
> many vases can she fill?
>
> **11 + 7 = 18 flowers**
> **18 ÷ 3 = 6 vases**

1. Mary buys 6 petunias and 8 marigolds. If she plants 2 in each pot, how many pots does she need?

2. Lucy has 19 pansies, 12 geraniums, and 5 marigolds. If she divides the flowers equally between 3 flower pots, how many flowers will each pot have?

3. Eric has 35 bags of fertilizer. He uses 5 bags of fertilizer on each lawn he fertilizes. How many lawns can he fertilize? If he earns $1.25 for each lawn he fertilizes, how much does he earn?

4. Kaylee buys 48 flowers. She puts 6 flowers in each vase. If she sells each vase for $2.35, how much does she earn?

© RBP Books

Party Planning

Solve each problem.

Samantha bakes 252 cupcakes for her birthday party. She gives each guest a box with 4 cupcakes. How many boxes does she have?

```
       63 boxes
   4) 252
     -24
       12
      -12
        0
```

1. Jill buys 349 party favors for 7¢ each. How much does Jill spend?

2. Bill has 72 cans of soda in 6-packs. How many 6-packs does he have?

3. A bunch of 12 balloons costs $13.99. If Marissa buys 3 bunches, how much does she spend on balloons?

4. Vivian has 396 party hats in packages. Each package contains 6 hats. How many packages does Vivian have?

46

Party Planning

Solve each problem.

1. Amanda hangs up decorations. She has 224 inches of ribbon and needs to cut 7-inch pieces. How many 7-inch pieces can she cut?

2. Carter brings 3 cakes. Each cake has 18 pieces. If there are 60 guests, will Carter have enough pieces? If not, how many more will he need?

3. Sean has 4 times as many guests at his party as Alex. Alex has 53 guests at his party. How many guests does Sean have?

4. Each person that came to Eric's party brought 3 gifts. Eric had 23 people come to his party. How many gifts did Eric get?

Did you know?

The largest cake every baked weighed more than 50 tons. It was baked in the shape of the state of Alabama.

Picture Problems

Color in the correct parts that are used for each fraction. Then write the fraction.

Remember...
The TOP part of the fraction tells how many parts you USE.
The BOTTOM part of the fraction tells how many parts THERE ARE.

Jada cut the pie into 6 pieces. Jada and her friends ate 3 pieces.

$$\frac{3}{6}$$

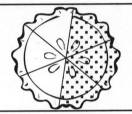

1. Brandon had 12 stickers. He gave 7 stickers to his friends.

2. The pepperoni pizza has 6 slices. Alex eats 4 slices.

3. Randy has 8 marbles. He loses 5 of the marbles when they roll down a crack in the sidewalk.

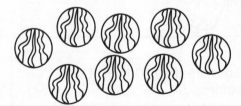

4. Karen has 9 chocolate kisses. She gives 6 chocolate kisses to her mom.

Pizza Party

Rob and his friends are making pizzas for their party. Help them solve the following problems.

First, Rob puts $\frac{3}{4}$ cup of flour in a bowl for the pizza dough. Then he adds another $\frac{1}{4}$ cup of flour. How much flour did he put in the dough?

$\frac{3}{4} + \frac{1}{4} = \frac{4}{4}$ **or 1 cup of flour**

1. Marcy rolls out the pizza dough. She uses $\frac{1}{2}$ cup. Then she adds another $\frac{1}{2}$ cup to make the pizza larger. How many cups did she use altogether?

2. Jan chops $\frac{1}{3}$ cup of mushrooms. She likes mushrooms, so she chops another $\frac{2}{3}$ cup. How many cups of mushrooms did she chop?

3. Lexie puts $\frac{3}{6}$ tablespoon of tomato sauce on the pizza. Then she adds $\frac{2}{6}$ tablespoon of tomato sauce. How much tomato sauce did she put on the pizza altogether?

4. John grates $\frac{3}{8}$ cup of cheese. Then he grates another $\frac{4}{8}$ cup of cheese. How much cheese did John grate altogether?

At the Park

Solve each problem. The first problem is worked for you.

Beth sees some ants crawling toward her picnic basket. $\frac{9}{16}$ of the ants are black. $\frac{7}{16}$ of the ants are red. How many more black ants are there than red ants?

$\frac{9}{16} - \frac{7}{16} = \frac{2}{16}$ **more black ants**

1. In the park, $\frac{3}{5}$ of the trees were elm trees. $\frac{2}{5}$ of the trees were oak trees. How many more elm trees were there than oak trees in the park?

2. Les had $\frac{8}{8}$ of a bottle of soda. He drank $\frac{4}{8}$ of the bottle. How much does Les have left?

3. Jasmine runs $\frac{3}{4}$ of a mile. Dan runs $\frac{1}{4}$ of a mile less than Jasmine. How far does Dan run?

4. Alex watches kites flying. $\frac{7}{16}$ of the kites are red, and $\frac{9}{16}$ of the kites are blue. How many more blue kites than red kites are there?

50

Solve each problem.

1. Jan puts $\frac{2}{16}$ cup of pepperoni on the pizza. Then she adds another $\frac{8}{16}$ cup of pepperoni. How much pepperoni is on the pizza?

2. Marcy adds $\frac{1}{6}$ teaspoon of pepper to the pizza. Then she adds $\frac{4}{6}$ teaspoon of pepper. How much pepper did she use on the pizza?

3. Max and Darla fly their kites. Max's kite flies $\frac{5}{4}$ of a yard. Darla's kite flies $\frac{2}{4}$ of a yard less than Max's kite. How many yards did Darla's kite fly?

Anyone ready for 1/6 of a pizza?

4. Adam brings $\frac{2}{3}$ of a pound of candy to the park. He shares $\frac{1}{3}$ of a pound of candy with his friends. How much candy does he have left?

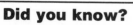

Did you know?

In 1903, Samuel Franklin Cody became the first person to cross the English Channel towed by a kite.

Painting Perfect

Solve each problem.

Rich bought $\frac{5}{16}$ quart of white paint and $\frac{11}{16}$ quart of blue paint. How much more blue paint did Rich buy?

$$\begin{array}{r} \frac{11}{16} \\ - \frac{5}{16} \\ \hline \frac{6}{16} \end{array}$$ **quart blue paint**

1. Heidi bought a gallon of paint. She needs $\frac{3}{4}$ of a gallon to paint her garage door. She spills $\frac{2}{4}$ of a gallon of paint. How much more paint does Heidi need to buy so she will have enough?

2. Mitch mixes $\frac{6}{8}$ of a quart of pink paint with $\frac{1}{8}$ of a quart of white paint. How much paint does he end up with?

3. Maria is at the paint store buying paintbrushes. She notices that $\frac{7}{10}$ of the paintbrushes are large, and $\frac{3}{10}$ of the paintbrushes are small. How many more large paintbrushes are there than small paintbrushes?

4. Daisy needs $\frac{8}{12}$ of a quart of paint to paint her backyard fence. She buys 1 quart of paint at the paint store. How much paint will Daisy have left?

Cookie Cutters

Tyler and his friends are making cookies for their party. Help them solve the problems below.

Debbie measures $\frac{1}{8}$ teaspoon of salt. She adds another $\frac{1}{8}$ teaspoon of salt. If her recipe calls for $\frac{5}{8}$ teaspoon of salt, how much more salt does she need to add?

$$+\begin{array}{r}\frac{1}{8}\\[2pt]\frac{1}{8}\\\hline\frac{2}{8}\end{array}\qquad -\begin{array}{r}\frac{5}{8}\\[2pt]\frac{2}{8}\\\hline\frac{3}{8}\end{array}$$ **teaspoons**

1. Kyle measures $\frac{1}{4}$ cup of flour. He adds another $\frac{1}{4}$ cup of flour. If his recipe calls for $\frac{3}{4}$ cup of flour, how much more flour does Kyle need to add?

2. Denise has $\frac{4}{6}$ tablespoon of baking soda in a dish. She puts $\frac{1}{6}$ tablespoon of that baking soda in her cookie dough. She adds another $\frac{2}{6}$ tablespoon. How much baking soda is left in her dish?

3. Tyler measures $\frac{5}{8}$ cup chocolate chips. He eats $\frac{1}{8}$ cup. He measures another $\frac{2}{8}$ cup. How many chocolate chips does he have left?

4. Sheena has $\frac{5}{4}$ cups of sugar in her container. She removes $\frac{2}{4}$ cup and then removes another $\frac{1}{4}$ cup. How much sugar is left in her sugar container?

Popsicles™

Answer the following questions using the graph below.

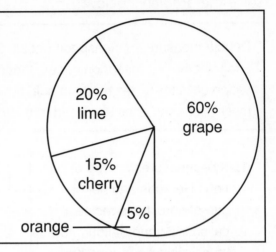

Third-Grade Students' Favorite Popsicle™ Flavors

This is a pie chart. It shows the favorite flavors of Popsicle™ for the third graders at Viewmont Elementary School.

20% lime

60% grape

15% cherry

5%

orange

1. What is the favorite flavor of Popsicle™ for third-grade students?

2. How many more students like grape Popsicles™ best than like orange Popsicles™?

3. What is the students' least favorite flavor of Popsicle™?

4. What percent of students like cherry or lime Popsicles™?

Answer the following questions using the graph below.

<u>Points Scored at the Playoff Game</u>

This is a bar graph. There is one bar for each person. Teresa and her friends played in the playoff basketball game for their school. The graph shows how many points they earned for their team.

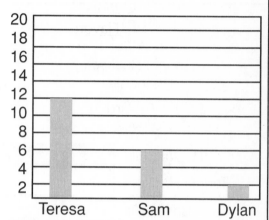

1. How many points did Sam score? _____

2. How many more points did Teresa score than Dylan? _____

3. How many points did Sam, Teresa, and Dylan score altogether? _____

4. How many points are represented by each line across the bar graph? _____

Word Problems Grade 3—RBP0709

Graph It!

The chart below shows the number of items sold at Sporty's Sporting Goods store. Put the information in a bar graph.

Item	Number Sold
Basketballs	18
Tennis Rackets	15
Baseballs	12
Bats	12
Gloves	6

Basketballs	
Tennis Rackets	
Baseballs	
Bats	
Gloves	

2   4   6   8   10   12   14   16   18

Use the bar graph to answer the questions.

1. How many tennis rackets were sold?

2. Which two items had equal numbers sold?

3. How many more basketballs than baseballs were sold?

4. How many more tennis rackets than gloves were sold?

56

Graph It!

Allie asked each class member what type of pet he or she has.
Record the results on the bar graph below.

Type of Pet	Number of Students
Dog	9
Goldfish	7
Cat	6
Lizard	3
No Pet	2
Turtle	1

Dog
Goldfish
Cat
Lizard
No Pet
Turtle

1 2 3 4 5 6 7 8 9 10

Use the bar graph to answer the questions.

1. What type of pet do the most students in the class have?

2. How many students have a lizard?

3. What is the least popular pet in the class?

4. What is the second most popular pet in the class?

Word Problems Grade 3—RBP0709

Up, Up, and Away

Figure out the travel times for each of the flight numbers. Then solve each problem using the information in the table.

Flight Number	Departure	Arrival	Travel Time
1	6:45 a.m.	8:00 a.m.	1 hour 15 minutes
2	9:00 a.m.	11:00 a.m.	
3	1:00 p.m.	3:30 p.m.	
4	4:45 p.m.	9:15 p.m.	
5	5:00 p.m.	10:00 p.m.	

1. Laura is trying to decide between taking flight 1 or flight 2. How much time will she save if she takes flight 1?

2. Bob takes flight 2 and then flight 3. How much time does Bob spend flying altogether?

Up, Up, and Away

Solve each problem using the information in the table on page 58.

1. Beth takes flights 2, 3, and 5 to get to her destination. How much time does she spend flying altogether?

2. Rick takes flight 4. Denise takes flight 5. Who has the shorter flying time?

3. Taylor takes flight 1. His flight arrives 30 minutes later than the arrival time. Emily takes flight 3. Her flight arrives 15 minutes earlier than the arrival time. Who spent longer flying, Taylor or Emily?

4. Mandy takes flight 5, and her sister takes flight 4. How much more time does Mandy spend flying than her sister?

Did you know?

The busiest airport in the world is Hartsfield in Atlanta, Georgia. Over 70 million people a year pass through the airport.

Through the Hoop

Solve each problem using the information in the line graph.

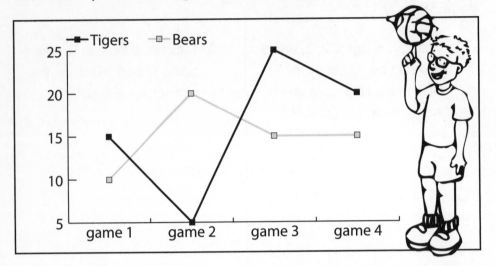

1. What was the average number of points the Bears scored for their first 3 games?

2. Which team scored the most points during the season?

3. How many more points did the Bears score in the first 2 games than the Tigers?

4. For games 1 and 2, which team scored the most points in all?

Solve each problem. The first problem is worked for you.

Remember...
The perimeter is the distance around a figure. To find the perimeter of a figure, add up the lengths of each side of the figure.

3"

3"   **3"**

3"

3+3+3+3=12

---

1. Blake is fencing a dog pen. Two of the sides are 67 feet, and the other two sides are 41 feet. How much fencing will Blake need? If fencing costs $.06 per foot, how much will Blake spend?

2. Anna is buying trim to go around her rug. Her rug measures 54 inches by 42 inches. If the trim costs 5 cents per inch, how much will Anna spend on trim?

3. Heather and Kim are sewing trim around their blankets. Heather's blanket measures 36 inches by 30 inches. Kim's blanket measures 42 inches by 28 inches. Who will need to buy more trim, Heather or Kim? How much more trim will she need?

4. Ben needs enough ribbon to go around the edge of his kite. Two of the edges are 15 inches, and the other two are 29 inches. How much ribbon will Ben need to buy? If ribbon costs 7 cents an inch, how much will Ben spend?

Misha and her friends are working at the community center. Help them solve the problems below.

Remember...
To find the area of a rectangular figure, multiply the length by the width. Give your answer in square units.

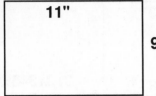

11"

9"

9 x 11 = 99 square inches

1. Misha and Matt are painting an area that is 12 feet by 8 feet. How many pints of paint will they need to buy if 1 pint covers 3 square feet?

2. Annie is carpeting 2 rooms. The first room is 17 feet by 13 feet, and the second room measures 32 feet by 14 feet. How many square feet of carpet will Annie need to buy?

3. Gary plants grass seed in an area behind the community center that is 8 feet wide and 9 feet long. If 1 bag of grass seed covers 3 square feet, how many bags of grass seed will Gary need?

4. Jess is repairing 2 windows. The first window measures 36 inches by 21 inches. The second measures 43 inches by 31 inches. How many square inches of glass will Jess need in all?

Fun at the Fair

Solve each problem. The first problem is worked for you.

Meg sold 8,397 tickets at the fair. Sam sold 5 times as many tickets as Meg. How many tickets did Sam sell?

```
  1 4 3
  8,397
x     5
41,985 tickets
```

1. There were 69 jars of pickles at the pickle-judging contest. Each jar had 9 pickles in it. How many pickles were there altogether?

2. The state fair is open for 9 weeks. How many days is that?

3. Mitch buys a soda for $1.45 and a hamburger for $3.54. He pays with a 10-dollar bill. How much change does Mitch get back?

4. The Twist-a-Whirl has 15 cars. Each car holds 4 people. How many people can ride the Twist-a-Whirl at a time?

63

Fun at the Fair

Solve each problem.

1. Janice sold 7 times as many packages of cotton candy as Tim. Tim sold 3,295 packages of cotton candy. How many packages of cotton candy did Janice sell?

2. The fair closes at 10:45. Karen checks her watch at 9:15 to see if she has time to ride the Ferris wheel. How much time does Karen have left before the fair closes?

3. Matt buys a toy car for $7.32 and a T-shirt for $15.39. How much money does Matt spend altogether?

4. The kiddie coaster holds 28 people. If 2 people can ride in a car, how many cars are there?

Did you know?
The fastest roller coaster in the world travels at over 100 miles per hour.

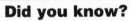

Sports Store Sales

Solve each problem. The first problem is worked for you.

The coach buys 5 times as many soccer balls as basketballs. He buys 6 basketballs. How many more soccer balls than basketballs does the coach buy?	6 **x 5** **30 soccer balls** 30 **– 6** **24 soccer balls**

1. The Sports-R-Us store sells 3 times more basketballs than baseballs. They sell 6 baseballs. How many more basketballs than baseballs do they sell?

2. Stephanie spends 4 times more on her tennis racket than she spends on running shoes. If she spends $54.88 on running shoes, how much does she spend altogether?

3. Dennis counted 9 times more footballs as soccer balls in the store. He counted 7 soccer balls. How many footballs and soccer balls did he count altogether?

4. In the winter season, the Sports-R-Us store sells 8 times more snowboards than during the summer season. The store sells 32 snowboards in the summer season. How many more snowboards does the store sell in the winter season than the summer season?

Sports Store Sales

Solve each problem.

1. Grace is checking her inventory. She has 7 times more scooters than skateboards. If she has 88 skateboards, how many scooters and skateboards does she have altogether?

2. The Sports-R-Us store sold 8 times as many soccer balls in May as in June. The store sold 162 soccer balls in June. How many soccer balls were sold altogether?

3. Jasmine sold 6 times more bicycle helmets than bicycles. She sold 124 bicycles. How many bicycle helmets and bicycles did she sell altogether?

4. Peter spent 4 times as much on his baseball bat than on his baseball. If he spent $16.98 for his baseball, how much did he spend altogether?

Did you know?

The modern skateboard was developed in 1958. The "Ollie" was invented in 1978 by Alan "Ollie" Gelfand.

Sweet Treats

Solve each problem.

Cassie has 11 jawbreakers, 14 gumdrops, and 29 jellybeans. If she divides her candy equally between 3 friends, how many pieces will each friend get?

$$\begin{array}{r} 11 \\ 14 \\ +\ 29 \\ \hline 54 \end{array}$$

$$3\overline{)54} = \textbf{18 pieces}$$

---

1. Leslie has 7 times as many chocolate doughnuts as plain doughnuts. She has 12 plain doughnuts. How many doughnuts does Leslie have altogether?

2. Marie has 5 times as many pieces of licorice as jelly-beans. She has 24 jelly-beans. How many more pieces of licorice than jelly-beans does Marie have?

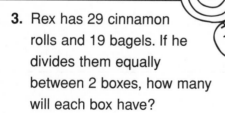

3. Rex has 29 cinnamon rolls and 19 bagels. If he divides them equally between 2 boxes, how many will each box have?

4. The Muffin Mania bakery sold 14 blueberry muffins, 9 spice muffins, and 7 bran muffins. If they put the same number of muffins in 6 boxes, how many muffins are in each box?

Word Problems Grade 3—RBP0709

Tiny-Tykes Toy Sales

The Tiny-Tykes toy store is finishing their yearly inventory. Help them figure out how many toys they have in their inventory by organizing the information in the table below.

There are 12 trains.

There are 6 times as many cars as trains.

There are 11 fewer trucks than cars.

There are 16 more games than trains.

There are 2 times as many stuffed animals as dolls.

There are 9 times as many dolls as games.

Toy:	How many:
trains	
games	
stuffed animals	
cars	
dolls	
trucks	

Tiny-Tykes Toy Sales

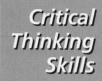
Work each problem. Use the information in the table on page 68.

1. If the store sells 104 stuffed animals and 72 dolls, how many stuffed animals and dolls are left altogether?

2. If the store sells all of their cars for 5 cents each and all of their trucks for 8 cents each, how much money will they make in all?

3. The store's inventory shows a total of 950 toys in the store. How many toys are not listed in the table?

4. How many more stuffed animals were sold than toy cars and trucks?

Word Problems Grade 3—RBP0709

Class Pets

The students at Edgemont School took a survey on the types of pets they have. Figure out how many students have each type of pet. Make a table to help organize the information.

Six students have a cat.

Nine times as many students have a dog as have a cat.

Three more students have a bird than have a dog.

Eighteen more students have a gerbil than have a guinea pig.

Twelve fewer students have a guinea pig than have a bird.

Ten fewer students have a fish than have a gerbil.

Pet:	Number of votes:
cats	
fish	
guinea pigs	
birds	
gerbils	
dogs	

Class Pets

Work each problem. Use the information in the table on page 70.

1. If 450 students voted, how many students do not have any pets?

2. How many more students voted for dogs and cats than voted for fish?

3. The students at Oakview School have 6 times as many dogs for pets as the students at Edgemont School. How many more students at Oakview own dogs?

4. Perky Pets pet store sold 6 times more bags of dog food than cat food. If the store sold 524 bags of cat food, how many bags of dog and cat food did the store sell in all?

In the News!

Read each problem carefully, and decide which information is needed to solve it. Then work each problem.

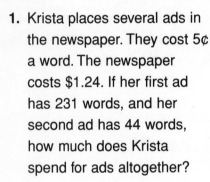

1. Krista places several ads in the newspaper. They cost 5¢ a word. The newspaper costs $1.24. If her first ad has 231 words, and her second ad has 44 words, how much does Krista spend for ads altogether?

2. Mark spends 3 times as much money at the news-stand as Zoe. Zoe spends $7.48. Mark buys 4 news-papers. How much more money does Mark spend than Zoe?

3. The *Daily Times* sells 491 papers for 4¢ each. The *City Globe* sells 299 papers for 6¢ each. They also sell magazines for $1.67. How much more does the *Daily Times* make from papers than the *City Globe?*

4. Kevin delivers 14 news-papers. Derrick delivers 12 more newspapers than Kevin. Kevin and Derrick get paid $.25 for each paper they deliver. Derrick buys a scooter for $27.98. How much more money does Derrick earn than Kevin?

In the News!

Read each problem carefully, and decide which information is needed to solve it. Then work each problem.

1. Garret delivers 125 newspapers. Allison delivers 5 times more newspapers than Garret. Allison buys 12 magazines. How many more newspapers does Allison deliver than Garret?

2. Julian buys a newspaper for $3.25 and a magazine for $11.39. He gives the clerk $15.00. He borrowed $4.00 from his friend. How much change does Julian get back?

3. Caroline buys 4 newspapers for $3.55 each. She also buys a special edition newspaper for $6.79. A magazine costs $3.79. How much money does Caroline spend altogether?

4. Courtney gets paid 4¢ for each word she writes. Her first article has 439 words. Her second article has 832 words, and her third article has 593 words. A newspaper costs $3.18. How much money does Courtney earn altogether?

At the Carnival

Read each problem, and decide if you have enough information to solve it. If there is enough information, solve the problem.

1. Marianne buys cotton candy for $1.85 and tickets for $8.49. How much change does she get back?

2. Carl buys 5 tickets for $.69 each and a snow cone for $1.49. He gives the cashier $10.00. How much change does he get back?

3. Rosa rides the crazy coaster 17 times. One ride on the crazy coaster takes 4 tickets. If tickets cost 7¢ each, how much does Rosa spend on crazy coaster rides?

4. Alex buys 2 T-shirts and a slice of pizza. A slice of pizza costs $1.39. How much does Alex spend altogether?

Answer Pages

Page 3
1. 26 fewer guppies
2. 120 goldfish
3. 14 plants
4. 86 goldfish

Page 4
1. 58 comets
2. 42 guppies
3. 99 snails
4. Tanner has 48 shrimp.
   They have 121 shrimp in all.

Page 5
1. Answers will vary.
2. Answers will vary.
3. Answers will vary.
4. Answers will vary.

Page 6
1. 5,868 tickets
2. 712 packages
3. 502 tickets
4. 469 seats

Page 7
1. Answers will vary.
2. Answers will vary.
3. 713 buckets
4. 419 tickets

Page 8
1. 16 ham sandwiches
2. 61 items in all, 6 bags of chips
3. 22 loaves
4. 17

Page 9
1. 4 cages
2. 4 snakes
3. 7 pounds
4. 45 people

Page 10
1. 19 gallons
2. 13 snakes
3. 30 pounds
4. 23 pictures

Page 11
1. 61 papers
2. 845 pencils
3. 446 students
4. 23 students

Page 12
1. 118 people voted
2. 203 orange backpacks
3. 15 students
4. 1,509 science books

Page 13
1. 70 calories
2. 590 calories

Page 14
1. 66 calories
2. 261 calories
3. 113 calories
4. a hamburger

Answer Pages

Page 15
1. 18 inches
2. 27° F
3. 15 miles per hour
4. 19° F

Page 16
1. 4,410 square miles
2. 2,142 feet
3. 155 feet
4. 3,428 square miles

Page 17
1. 3,462 feet
2. 434 miles long
3. 137 more endangered plants
4. 2,184 square kilometers

Page 18
1. 198 students
2. 564 students
3. 1,262 students
4. 1,236 students

Page 19
1. $4.41
2. $7.85
3. $8.63
4. Yes; he has $.95 left.

Page 20
1. $1.10
2. $4.73
3. $9.86
4. $2.12

Page 21
1. $3.21
2. $131.80
3. $2.69
4. $23.48

Page 22
1. $6.50
2. $4.98
3. $2.30
4. $0.06

Page 23
1. $8.52
2. $11.22
3. $8.57
4. $3.55

Page 24
1. 28 people
2. 6 feet
3. 21 bottles of water
4. 36 wildebeest

Page 25
1. 36 tires
2. 54 keys
3. 56 trucks
4. 40 red cars

Page 26
1. 24 tents
2. 12 sport utility vehicles
3. 21 miles
4. 18 bottles

Answer Pages

Page 27
1. 84 red pet collars
2. 42 lettuce leaves
3. 39 poodles
4. 48 bags of seed

Page 28
1. 235 tomato plants
2. 102 gallons
3. 92 bags of fertilizer
4. 115 lawns

Page 29
1. 96 times
2. 69 dog toys
3. 111 garden tools
4. 354 squashes

Page 30
1. 620 gallons of paint
2. 196 feet
3. 1,504 paintbrushes
4. No; she has only 105 liters.

Page 31
1. 2,296 people
2. 4,752 magazines
3. 1,401 books
4. 2,848 books

Page 32
1. 7 seashells per box
2. 343 fish
3. 186 seashells
4. 180 feet

Page 33
1. 435 fish
2. 168 feet
3. 146 sea creatures
4. 266 fish

Page 34
1. $3.60
2. Yes; he has $13.50.
3. $10.50
4. (Answers will vary.)
   1 ten-dollar bill, 1 one-dollar bill,
   3 quarters, and 1 penny

Page 35
1. $31.00
2. $2.83
3. No; she only has $8.60.
4. (Answers will vary.)
   1 ten-dollar bill, 1 five-dollar bill,
   2 one-dollar bills, 1 quarter, 1 dime,
   1 nickel and 3 pennies

Page 36
1. 207¢ or $2.07
2. 768¢ or $7.68
3. 95¢ or $0.95
4. 876¢ or $8.76

Page 37
1. $126.00
2. 445¢ or $4.45
3. 228¢ or $2.28
4. 711¢ or $7.11

Page 38
1. 3,470¢ or $34.70
2. $23.75
3. 13,964¢ or $139.64
4. $2.10

© RBP Books

Answer Pages

Page 39
1. Erica $20.94, Alex $31.00, Alex
2. Sam $31.41, Liz $21.25, Sam

Page 40
1. Jessica $16.63, Isaac $27.99, Isaac
2. Lance $18.49, Mitch $23.47, Mitch
3. Penny $40.15, Jackson $50.49, Jackson
4. Megan $25.95, Marcy $17.43, Megan

Page 41
1. 7:45
2. 10:15
3. 9:15
4. 7:45

Page 42
1. 5 pieces each
2. 8 candy bars
3. 6 gumdrops
4. 6 packages

Page 43
1. 47 campers
2. 76 flashlights
3. 84 sandwiches
4. 73 backpacks

Page 44
1. 46 pieces of string
2. 65 days
3. 27 tents
4. 36 campers

Page 45
1. 7 pots
2. 12 flowers
3. 7 lawns, $8.75
4. $18.80

Page 46
1. 2,443¢ or $24.43
2. 12 6-packs
3. $41.97
4. 66 packages

Page 47
1. 32 pieces of ribbon
2. No. He has 54 pieces, so he will need 6 more pieces.
3. 212 guests
4. 69 gifts

Page 48

1. $\frac{7}{12}$

2. $\frac{4}{6}$

3. $\frac{5}{8}$

4. $\frac{6}{9}$

Page 49
1. $\frac{2}{2}$ or 1 cup
2. $\frac{3}{3}$ or 1 cup
3. $\frac{5}{6}$ tablespoon
4. $\frac{7}{8}$ cup

Answer Pages

Page 50
1. $\frac{1}{5}$ more elm trees
2. $\frac{4}{8}$ of a bottle
3. $\frac{2}{4}$ of a mile
4. $\frac{2}{16}$ more blue kites

Page 51
1. $\frac{10}{16}$ cup
2. $\frac{5}{6}$ teaspoon
3. $\frac{3}{4}$ yard
4. $\frac{1}{3}$ pound

Page 52
1. $\frac{1}{4}$ gallon
2. $\frac{7}{8}$ quart
3. $\frac{4}{10}$ more large paintbrushes
4. $\frac{4}{12}$ quart

Page 53
1. $\frac{1}{4}$ cup
2. $\frac{1}{6}$ tablespoon
3. $\frac{2}{8}$ or $\frac{1}{4}$ cup
4. $\frac{2}{4}$ or $\frac{1}{2}$ cup

Page 54
1. grape
2. 55%
3. orange
4. 35%

Page 55
1. 6 points
2. 10 more points
3. 20 points
4. 2 points

Page 56
1. 15 tennis rackets
2. baseballs and bats
3. 6 more basketballs
4. 9 more tennis rackets

Page 57
1. dog
2. 3 students
3. turtle
4. goldfish

Page 58
1. 45 minutes
2. 4 hours and 30 minutes

Page 59
1. 9 hours and 30 minutes
2. Rick
3. Emily
4. 30 minutes

Page 60
1. 15 points
2. Tigers
3. 10 points
4. Bears

Page 61
1. 216 feet, $12.96
2. $9.60
3. Kim, 8 inches more
4. 88 inches, $6.16

Answer Pages

Page 62
1. 32 pints
2. 669 square feet of carpet
3. 24 bags of grass seed
4. 2,089 square inches of glass

Page 63
1. 621 pickles
2. 63 days
3. $5.01
4. 60 people

Page 64
1. 23,065 packages
2. 1 hour and 30 minutes
3. $22.71
4. 14 cars

Page 65
1. 12 basketballs
2. $274.40
3. 70 balls
4. 224 snowboards

Page 66
1. 704 scooters and skateboards
2. 1,458 soccer balls
3. 868 bicycles and helmets
4. $84.90

Page 67
1. 96 doughnuts
2. 96 more pieces
3. 24 items per box
4. 5 muffins in each box

Page 68
1. 12 trains
2. 28 games
3. 504 stuffed animals
4. 72 cars
5. 252 dolls
6. 61 trucks

Page 69
1. 580 stuffed animals and dolls
2. $8.48
3. 21 toys
4. 371 stuffed animals

Page 70
1. 6 cats
2. 53 fish
3. 45 guinea pigs
4. 57 birds
5. 63 gerbils
6. 54 dogs

Page 71
1. 172 students
2. 7 students
3. 270 students
4. 3,668 bags of dog and cat food

Page 72
1. $13.75
2. $14.96
3. $1.70
4. $3.00

Page 73
1. 500 newspapers
2. $.36
3. $20.99
4. $74.56

Page 74
1. not enough information
2. $5.06
3. $4.76
4. not enough information

www.summerbridgeactivities.com